Recollections of My Soul

Chiara Laricchiuta

AOS PUBLISHING, 2023

AOS POETRY, 2023

ISBN: 978-1-990496-12-7

Cover Design: Antonietta D'Amore

Visit AOS Publishing's website:
www.aospublishing.com

Dedicated to two of the most important people in my life, the one who taught me the true meaning of love, grace and elegance, the origin of my life, my mother, Nina. And to my late father, Gerry, who in his unique way, taught me how to be strong and how to embrace life with all its twists and turns. I learned so much from my parents, and I made mistakes of my own and I learned some more. Through all the light and the darkness, this collection has emerged, and it has set my soul free.

I would like to thank my mother, Nina and my sisters, Rosa and Nelly for their unconditional love and support. You have always been incredible role models.

I would also like to thank my loving husband, Anthony, for his encouragement, his profound understanding of creating art and for allowing me a safe space to share so much of myself freely.

Most importantly, to the light of my life, my daughter, Valesca, who continues to inspire me every day through her innocence and kindness. She gives me strength, warmth, and the courage to touch the stars.

A very special thank you to AOS publishing for believing in my work and for giving me this remarkable opportunity. You have helped me achieve a lifelong dream.

"Writing not only feeds my spirit but it has always been a cathartic experience for me. It has helped me overcome so many personal hardships, it has allowed me to revel and revisit my joys but most of all it has given my soul a voice."

Contents

Reflections

Author's Note

A collection of intimate poems spanning over two decades in which I address the universal themes of love, death, suffering, coping with loss and a nostalgic homage to youth and childhood. They are themes everyone can relate to. Every poem tells a fragment of a story. These poems are meant to evoke emotions in the reader and leave a legacy of words that will immortalize the human spirit and fill it with passion and an eternal inspiration to create.

The first part of this compilation is a collection of poems. The second part is a section of short reflections.

Alone

The perpetual rise and fall,
The one breasted lady in my dreams, walking
awkwardly toward a beautiful babe,
Familiar faces from the past saluting and lamenting, not
sure where they are going,
White worms crawling in different directions, trying to
escape the elusive wallpaper,
The critical mind as sharp as a blade, legs as heavy as
cement, slowing everything down,
Trying to press reset or escape but nothing is
happening, nothing stops, until it all does.

Beyond Absolutes

Thinking too much, thinking too little,
not thinking at all.
I think therefore I exist,
I overthink therefore I am not present,
I don't like to think therefore I am ignorant.
Ignorance is bliss, knowledge is sacred.
Glass half empty or glass half full?
Practice positive thinking for healing,
Self-affirmations are like vitamins,
The universe is talking to us every day,
We can't hear it. We are too busy doing this or that.
Let's listen deeply and with compassion,
We are all light and dark.
The magic is in the obscurities,
Things we cannot fully grasp, moments that
take our breath away,
What just happened? You've lived a life in haste, a life of
wasted time,
Consumed by worrying and relentless thoughts.
You lived like you were already dead, so stuck in narrow
constructs,
Ignoring all the signs, and all the subtle beauty that
exists in each moment.

Blissland

The clouds that you have left behind are parting,
There are no more tears to cry, the sun has dried them
all.
The shadows of your life have been lifted and the
rainbow is blinding the sky.
Your essence has vanished from this place.
Do you suffer and deafen Heaven with your cries?
I can't hear you. All I hear is an unfamiliar sound,
silence. I must go.
I cannot be late, my appointment with life is now.
I wish you well.

BLOCKED

Physically obstructed
Porous skin, bloated abdomen, chronic pain
Mental anxiety, fear is to blame
Captive thoughts and silent tongues
Unfulfilled dreams, fluttering ambition
Indecisive mind, scattered ideas,
Severing ties, stuck in time.

CONSUMED

Even if you are gone, you still dictate her life.
Her mind races in haste and she cannot find peace.
Moving on is like an impossible dream – a dead end.
Her body is paralyzed without you.
She agonizes about the past,
And only finds comfort, drowning in a pool of self-pity.
Her negativity consumes even the stars,
For her one wish, could only take a miracle.

DOUBT

It is planted by a callous thought
It grows from a contaminated seed and can spread
ferociously
Like a cancer, it eats away at you tirelessly
If you let it fester it poisons your soul and like a thief, it
robs pieces of you
It leaves you feeling spent and takes your breath away.
Be gentle with it like a mother is with her child,
Treat it with the same compassion you would show a
dear friend
You will disarm it with your feminine strength and like
the fluid viscosity of water it will delicately evaporate
into the mist.

Emotional Fraud

Invested time for falsified stories
Invested energy for impersonated feelings
Invested love for overdrawn lies
Invested hope for deceitful games
Invested desire for counterfeit flesh

Enchanted

The strong tree trunk resembling elephant skin
The cobblestone road is open wide, like the sky
The emerald, green grass is a comforting carpet
The passage of time marked by heavy roots bursting
from the fertile earth
A dried orange peel curled up in a sweetened slumber
Butterflies buried in deep caramel, desperate to taste
the decadent sap dwelling within the
forbidden fruit.

Eros

*You are the dark secret I keep hidden like a forbidden
taboo.*
Days are spent battling the demons of eros in my mind.
*Thoughts of your dark silhouette send shivers down my
spine.*
*My tongue has refrained itself from revealing the
workings of my heart,*
*Yet when our bodies collide, I am unable to arrest my
deepest desires.*
*Your eyes pierce through me and detect the
contradiction in my speech.*
*I convince myself that time will erase your voice from
my memory,*
*But desire reigns supreme and I crave to satisfy you
with the truth.*

Exposed

We try our best to hide it,
We bury it deep down,
In the dark recesses of our minds.
We think it is safe and hidden from the world.
But it's too brash. It makes us cry, it makes us tremble,
it makes us erupt like hot, thick, sticky lava for our
children to absorb.
We pass it down to innocent minds that
can't deal with it.
They can't sit still, they want more, they think they are
not enough.
They did not ask to be here.
We can't pretend they don't exist when they lash out
and our anguish is exposed.

Golden

Your heart is a treasure to adore and protect,
The goodness it holds I could never neglect.
It may be broken, fragile and meek
But know you have me when it's strength that you seek.
Only time will help mend it,
Of this, I am sure.
And while you are waiting, I can offer a cure:
Let go of what hurt you and set yourself free,
You will shine in your splendor
And the truth you will see.

I am Broken too

It's not only about you, it's about me too
If you help me, I can help you
We need to stop blaming each other
Can't we share this love we have and make it stronger?
All we do is go around in circles
No one is listening to the other
We both deserve love, let's give and take
Let's fix it together, be better for one another
I can't do it alone, I am broken too

I Choose Me

It's not my cross to carry,
It's a foreign wound to me,
You can't pass it on or ignore it,
To set yourself free,
Nothing is that easy.

The shortcuts you take, the excuses you make,
The kind words you hear but don't listen to,
All the traps of procrastination that stifle your
emancipation.

I'm not going down this painful road, what lesson will it
serve?
I'm not being selfish; I know what I deserve.
I am the judge, and I am the jury
I took my time and did the work,
And now, I have something to offer, without bearing
any burden.

To rid yourself of the excess weight **you** must do the
exercise,
It's about self-preservation, a life's journey of
understanding pain,
It's like unlocking the greatest treasure, and nothing
can get in your way,
no obstacle you can't surmount once you realize,

True Love lies within, it's not something you take.

If you could see us now

If you could see us now,
What would be the first thing you'd say?

If you could see us now,
And all the life we've lived, the paths we've carved
The love we nourished.

If you could see us now,
What happiness it would bring!
Would it be enough, could it ever be?

If you could see us now,
Would you recognize the treasures you helped create?
The ones you could never fully appreciate.

If you could see us now,
You would realize we still shine bright,
We were strong enough to survive the pain.

If you could see us now,
You would weep for days,
For the time you lost.
For the love you tossed.

If you could see us now,
We'd take your breath away.

In Ogni Senso

It leaves an everlasting mark,
A stain that cannot be removed by the stubborn strokes
of time,
It is a permanent scar that is delicately woven into the
chamber of your heart,
A scar that was once a bright star with so many
promises and reveries,
It shined so brilliantly, it made you believe in the magic
of the universe,
It may have faltered like a voice in your imagination, it
may have brought you closer to the angels,
For even a brief moment you were touched by the
splendor of LOVE.

In Ogni Senso (in Italiano)

Lascia un segno eterno,
Una macchia che non può essere rimossa dai colpi
ostinati del tempo,
È una cicatrice permanente che è delicatamente
intessuta nella camera del tuo cuore,
Una cicatrice che un tempo era una stella luminosa con
tante promesse e fantasticherie,
Brillava così brillantemente, ti faceva credere nella
magia dell'universo,
Potrebbe aver vacillato come una voce nella tua
immaginazione, potrebbe averti avvicinato agli angeli,
Anche per un breve momento sei stato toccato dallo
splendore dell'AMORE

Jane Doe

I am no longer my father's daughter.
Like a fictious character who existed for a short while,
Now a mere figment of my imagination.
Everything about him is gone, nothing is real.
It is an illusion, a fabrication, an abstraction
of a past life.
What does that make me?
Some girl with half an identity.

Killer instincts

Loud voice, closed mind
Patronizing air, veiled insecurities
Pretentious disposition, bleeding heart
Extravagant displays, lack of self-worth
Socially awkward, disconnected from reality
Overburdened with pride, fear of introspection
Moody and volatile, mentally unhinged
Overcritical and rigid, emotionally void
Devoid of culpability, narcissistic

Lazarus

Covered in ash
battered by men
who battled the snakes
abandoned by mothers
left to survive
like the renaissance of spring
a plethora of color
a revival of verve
the dead among the living
give rise to the light

Letting Go

I was so afraid of what I didn't know,
What I couldn't see, had such a hold on me.

I agonized about what might come,
It made my joy numb.

The tug of war inside of me was so deep,
I couldn't sleep.

Why did I allow this madness to exist?
What is it that I couldn't resist?

The answer I discovered, inside my soul was locked
In a secret gateway, I, myself, had blocked.

But the sun is shining brightly now,
As brightly as can be,

It has melted all the darkness,
And the light has set me free!

Love your shadow

We are all light and dark,
We are all triumphs and failures,
We all carry hopes and dreams, scars, and fears,
We must care for our pain,
We have so much to gain,
We can appreciate the rainbow in the sky and the
laughter of a child.
We must delicately talk to our sorrows and console
them,
Water the seeds of joy and light in us every day.
The dark is part of the light, it deserves care and love,
Once the dark and light unite and harmonize in peace,
the transformative power of love will bloom in you,
It will transcend beyond time and space, and your
energy, contagious and bright, will help heal the world
And you will be free.

My Quiet Place

Alone with my thoughts this evening,
I turn to that serene place deep within,
that takes me away, far from the city lights,
where all is calm, all is still.
Here I meditate on recollections of things past,
I dwell on sweet echoes of laughter and of
promises made in the dark that time has chased away.
As memories resonate through my mind, like sharp rays
of sunlight,
I can still feel the warmth, smell the freshness, and taste
the sweetness
of these my most cherished moments.
Only here can time stand still, only here in my quiet
place.

November

The rain drops and each drop is a tear,
There are so many drops pouring down in such haste
As those tears that slide down my cheeks
into a pool of sorrow.
The sky isn't dark. It is a frosty white, it is pure and
anxiously awaiting the sun,
As my heart yearns to be saved from this infinite
tempest that swims through my veins like water flowing
through uncontrollable rapids.

Old Friend

We sat on your porch for what felt like an eternity,
Thinking time would stand still for us,
Two sweet rebels, we made wild plans and broke some
hearts
We laughed about the past and we cried through our
sorrows
You held my hand and I held yours, knowing we would
always have each other
Things changed and time passed but never will I forget
the special bond we shared.

Origin of Love

I am quilted with peace and total serenity,
The labor of love lies deep within me.
Something so small, so precious, so true,
Has managed to capture my heart, that is you.
I need not see to know; I will love forever more.
For you have changed my life and made me better than
before.
I long to hold you in my arms and sing you this first
lullaby,
And next to mine, your soft tender heart will lie.

Out in the Storm without an Umbrella

That day you came to me,
You revealed the unthinkable with such conviction,
I was struck by lightning, my heart left there bleeding.
I know now it had nothing to do with me,
It was you who suffered deeply,
The hurt you carried all those years wore you down to pieces,
You couldn't share any love, so you shared your pain,
How could you help me if you were left out in the storm without an umbrella?

Perfection Dejection

Cover up that blemish it's so distasteful,
Quiet with that creative talk, it's no way to earn a living,
There's no time to entertain those people, you are better than them
Don't be so sensitive, displaying your emotions is not a classy thing to do
You have been molded to believe that status and rank reign supreme
You have adopted a cold, corporate state of mind
There is no time for mistakes, reach the highest standard, nothing else will do
Social class, competition and materialism are the norm in your circle now
Sometimes you contemplate: How will my vocation serve the greater good?
It doesn't matter, play the part, what matters is the big paycheck

Plastic Avatars

Look in the mirror, who do you see?
A warped version of reality.
Why do you fear the passage of time?
Those fine lines on a unique canvas that reveal a special story,
Your frenetic impulse to erase them like a mistake,
The wisdom you've acquired, unacknowledged.
The respect for time passed, unobserved.
This illusive ideal perpetuating an artificial expression of life.
Is your ego that frail?
Is the vanity that deep?
In the ripening fruit, you find grace, the tragedy is the distortion in the mirror.

Pockets of Sunshine

A flashing light,
Zesty lemon gloss,
A refurbished point of view,
Seasons of life,
Things that can't get replaced,
Millions of sorbet-colored smiles,
Dreaming through storms,
A labyrinth of love.

Praeterita

Leave me alone.
I thought I dealt with you.
You had your time, wasn't it enough?
You can't just barge in on me whenever you please!
You are not invited. It is my time now.
I want to be free from you, unshackle me.
I love you and I hate you.
If you love me, accept it and begone.

Praeterita (in Italiano)

Lasciami sola.
Pensavo di aver avuto a che fare con te.
Hai avuto il tuo tempo, non è stato abbastanza?
Non puoi semplicemente invadermi ogni volta che
vuoi!
Non sei invitato. È il mio momento adesso.
Voglio essere libera, liberami.
Ti amo e ti odio.
Se mi ami, accettalo e vattene.

Prima Patria

She wept and I couldn't understand,
She looked at pictures reliving each black and white
moment.
She wrote letters to ghosts who had forgotten who she
was.
She sang old anthems until she lost her voice.
With each verse, she remembered how the ocean had
swallowed all her dreams.
She felt naked in this new place called home even
when her hair turned silver.
We returned together to her birthplace and there I saw
my mother for the first time.
The olive trees caressed us as we walked along an
endless field.
She said she could hear the ocean calling her name.
I looked into her blue eyes as majestic as the summer
sky and I understood everything.

Prima Patria (in Italiano)

Lei piangeva e io non riuscivo a capire,
Guardava le immagini rivivendo ogni momento in
bianco e nero.
Scriveva lettere ai fantasmi che avevano dimenticato chi
fosse.
Ha cantato vecchi inni finché ha perso la voce.
Ad ogni verso, ricordava come l'oceano avesse
inghiottito tutti i suoi sogni.
Si sentiva nuda in questo nuovo posto chiamato casa,
anche quando i suoi capelli diventarono d'argento.
Siamo tornati insieme nella sua città natale e lì ho visto
mia madre per la prima volta.
Gli ulivi ci accarezzavano mentre camminavamo lungo
un campo infinito.
Ha detto che poteva sentire l'oceano chiamare il suo
nome.
Ho guardato nei suoi occhi azzurri maestosi come il
cielo estivo e ho capito tutto.

Dedicato a te mamma, per tutto l'amore e per avermi
trasmesso tanta passione
per creare un mondo solo mio in cui mi posso
esprimere senza limiti,
come il mare di Polignano, che vedo ogni volta che ti
guardo.

Purge

You dig deep enough so it hurts until you can't breathe
You make it hemorrhage out of you like a flowing river
You try to expel it from its root
It's been rotting there for too long
There is no shame in your suffering, your story is real
Accept your pain and embrace it with tenderness
It is part of who you are, it isn't who you are
You are not your emotions, you are not your pain
Every day you are changing, and it is beautiful
Every day you are closer to your true self.

Quick fix

I reach for you, and you make it all go away for a while,
You take me to that place that's just mine,
Far from here, where I need to be.
You never disappoint me, you never ask me why,
You are there for me night and day, no excuses.
You never judge me.
You let me take as much as I want and I crave you even more,
I want to use you until there is nothing left to feel.

Reconciliation

I wish you laughter to brighten all your days.
I wish you an open heart to take in all the warmth around you.
I wish you the innocent gaze of a child to appreciate the miracle of every moment.
I wish you great fulfilling adventures to awaken your senses.
I wish you the greatest love of all, self-love!

Retreat

Not existing but not dying,
Completely disconnected and light,
A foreigner to the universe,
Not needed, but loved,
Engulfed in peace,
Grasped without uttering a sound,
Sinking into a warm blanket away from the noise.

Saving Mirabilandia

Keep some just for you, guilt-free,
Like that secret stash of joy, you keep hidden for those
rainy days,
Like an old polaroid that jumps out of a vintage jacket
pocket that only you can appreciate,
Protect those tiny pieces of your soul, away from the
vultures to devour,
Some intimacies are too precious to share,
It's easy to get lost along the way,
It's a long and crazy ride.

Saving Mirabilandia (in Italiano)

Risparmiane un po' solo per te, senza sensi di colpa,
Come quella scorta segreta di gioia che tieni nascosta
per quei giorni di pioggia,
Come una vecchia polaroid che salta fuori dalla tasca di
una giacca vintage,
Tieni quei piccoli pezzi della tua anima su un piatto
d'argento lontano dagli avvoltoi da divorare,
Ci sono alcune intimità che sono troppo preziose per
essere condivise, nessuno vale così tanto, ma tu,
È facile perdersi lungo la strada,
È una corsa lunga e folle.

Strange Frequencies

I can't see it, but I feel it.
I can't prove it, but I know it.
It creeps up on me now and again like an unwanted guest,
Nuances that I can piece together intricately.
Pulsations and sensations,
Even if it's true what can I do?
All this worry and fear,
The narrative in my head,
It's all for naught.

Superior Funk

Your superior funk,
Your silent rhetoric,
Your hypercritical eye and condescending smile,
It makes the air thick and heavy, it makes the sun
cringe,
I see through your extravagant displays and hypocrisy,
I am not touched by your volatility,
It reeks of profound insecurity.

The Easter Card

A casual oversight
Months of erratic movements
A red turtleneck

A bold confrontation
A familiar sting
Unforgiving eyes

A sarcastic tone
Empty threats
An ironic smile

A relentless mission
An ocean of lies
A gross unraveling

The beginning of the end

The *"Good"* Life

Overflowing with money and buried in loneliness
Big lavish houses inhabited by broken hearts
Workaholic, sleep deprived beings, with no balance
Pornography to distract the restless mind
Overindulgence and conspicuous consumption filling a
myriad of voids
Fancy cars driven by empty souls
Expensive diamonds gifted to conceal dark secrets

The Journey

It begins with nothing and turns into something.
It ends with something and becomes nothing.
A speck of energy meant to take flight,
Noise, action, things, knowledge, emotions, people,
duties day after day.
A final release into silence, calm, slumber,
unknowingness, freedom.
A legacy of thoughts, actions and words remain for
eternity.
They make our ancestors proud,
They make our children strong,
It never really had a beginning or an end,
It continues changing.

The Miracle of Your Name

You are the one and only ever you
No matter your birthplace,
No matter your lineage,
You are so precious and unique.
No one has your story to tell, you are so brave.
Feel how the sun shines down on you, you are loved.
Listen to the birds, as they sing their glorious tune, you
are worthy.
Look up at the stars, they are shining for you, they
applaud your dreams.
Smell the flowers, let the perfume fill your spirit, you
are beautiful.
Touch the waterfall, it is there to wash away all your
inhibitions, you are free.
Whisper the sound of your name, you are a miracle.

The Poet

A lover of words and ancient places,
A bold character provoking raw emotion,
Perhaps too real for the faint of heart.
With an investigative spirit navigating the world,
seeing through disingenuous hearts.
A childlike enthusiasm exuding freedom and passion,
Disenchanted by artifice and ceremony,
Transforming words into stories,
With an ethereal connection to the workings of her
soul,
Sharing gifts with those who are open to what authentic
wealth brings.

Time

A frosted windowpane
Fading white powder
The smell of vanilla candle wax gently melting
memories

Water flowing in a fountain of peace
Yellow tulips smiling
A slow, calm rhythm existing in a quiet room

A lavender arm charm, embracing a delicate silhouette
Cedars standing tall as if waiting for a special guest
Soft whispers, tiny hands, the promise of tomorrow

Ton of BRICKS

Needy and negative,
All consuming,
Never satisfied,
Clingy and desperate,
Indecisive and fearful,
Lazy and manipulative,
Slow and laborious,
Yet impatient and easily moved,
Eternally relying on others for the solution,
You are the biggest obstacle in your way,
You know it but will never admit it,
Blame it all on the world,
Save your sob stories for the queen.

Unhinged

Suffocated by fear
Tormented with doubt
Unable to sleep
Clouded by visions and manifestations of a reckless act
The dagger runs deep, it permeates the soul
The air is thick, the smell is foul
The howling wind is the narrator of the tortured storm
Frailty is the poison you are forced to drink

Untitled

You have invaded my thoughts it seems,
And have made me drunk with fatigue.
Uninvitingly you present yourself in my dreams,
Occupying unchartered terrain, spilling excrements of intrigue.
I, taken by this folly am desperate to be set free,
But I reek of unsavory traces of your smell.
I am unable to run, your intoxicating presence suffocates me.
My eyes bleed in disbelief and swell,
As they are made witness to an unforgiving boldness.
Your untamed persistence devours any of my attempts to reject you,
And your chivalrous promise to plague me with happiness,
Torments me with the knowledge that,

You will always provoke me with shame
Like a lethal gas does a burning flame.

Where I want to be

*I lie awake aware – denial drowned itself in my ocean of
tears.
I acknowledge the sun as a warm entity – hate has been
exorcised from my soul.
I can watch a bird take its glorious flight – panic has
fled my house.
I indulge in each moment – I am no longer in search of
dismantled parts.
Painful memories from a cold and distant past resonate
like shadows in a vague dream
A time I can no longer remember, a past I feel no
longer a part of.
Acceptance becomes me.*

Wildfire

A spark in my heart has ignited,
there is little time to act.
Ghosts have come back to haunt me,
reminding me that youth has passed.
The seasons of life seem shorter now
and winter is drawing near.
The shackles of time have a hold on me,
but it is this urgency, I fear.
It is driven by desire and folly,
to relive moments gone by.
I sometimes lose track of direction,
yet frantically I try,
To redeem my losses and indulge in the moment,
for soon day will turn to night.
And I will be free of my yearnings,
for they will vanish in eternal light.

Winter

Darkness is upon you my friend, there is no escape.
The storm of winter has reached you; everything has stopped.
He has sent the raven to alert the village, he will sing a farewell song.
In the distance, shadows of a reaper appear, he is dressed in black, looking for your tombstone.
Your widow weeps as she rests a red rose near your casket, and they cover you
in muddy earth.
They leave you there in the middle of a barren field under a frozen tree.
One can never be fully prepared for the inevitable last dance.
Twas only yesterday we exchanged pleasantries and drank wine,
It sends shivers down my spine, knowing winter will soon come for me too.

Wolf

He walks cautiously with a magnetic aura,
A hauntingly charming and passionate presence.
His insatiable appetite knows no bounds.
His piercing eyes are perceptive and sharp.
They are camouflaged by pain that is seldom exposed,
His tenacious desire is to protect what he loves.

Womanhood

Some days you feel like a curse
A heavy burden I don't want to carry
All the expectations have me forlorn
I envy the ones that can escape them all
Those who are free from this mental prison
We are not able to do as we please, the guilt would
destroy us
We are too worried about those we might offend,
Those who rely on our elegance.
To show all our strength would be too much.
Those who rule the world can't bear us being anything
more,
They have forgotten who has given birth to them.

You Weren't Supposed to Be Here

You weren't supposed to be here,
I was afraid when I found out.
We lived far away that year.
I worried and filled my mind with doubt.
You weren't supposed to be here,
I prayed silently for you to disappear,
But you grew stronger and your heartbeat faster,
And it appeased my fear.
You weren't supposed to be here,
Then I saw your precious face,
and I knew those feelings I felt were not real,
they were things I never said,
mere impressions in my head.

Young Hearts

The smell of wood burning on a warm summer night,
The perfect blend of a yellow and orange spectacle
melting in the sky,
The taste of the sea on a cushion of cool lips,
The radio incessantly buzzing that special tune,
The one that is forever etched in your heart.
The incredible feeling of invincibility,
The beauty of being oblivious to time who hasn't
become a thief yet,
Lavish dreams that seem effortless to attain,
Like a crisp, juicy apple ready to be plucked from a
blossoming tree.
The immutable conviction that everything will be
immortalized in this perfect moment.
The sweet innocence of young hearts.

Zomig

Heavy bricks and a million thorns
Light is the enemy and noise is his ally
Daggers and zaps infiltrating the brain
Am I the child, the girl, or the woman?
Useless and numb, a dead weight
A paralyzed existence, wiped off the map
Cancel my day, maybe my week
In the abyss of a dark room, all alone
Where is my mother? She used to make it better
A familiar metallic taste and a pounding heart
Trying to make sense of yesterday and tomorrow
Tears smear the frost-bitten pillow
Waiting for the cold sting of pain to pass
How long have I been here?
The gift of relief wrapped up in that long lethargic feeling

Making Sense of the Chaos
(Inspired by Plato's Allegory of the Cave)

If a man has been in a dark cave his whole life, believing his own reality to be the shadows (lies, and constructs made up by others around him) he cannot see the light (the sun, the truth), he resists it, he refuses it. Part of the refusal or rejection that impedes his growth involves: not accepting good advice, avoiding self-examination to allow self-healing, not owning up to his own flaws, dismissing apologies, or refraining from apologizing. His only comfort lies in diffusing the responsibility by blaming others and making excuses about his own limitations. He seeks pleasure in criticizing others because of his own inadequacies. He moves forward on a dark, negative path and tries to fill his void through vices. The only way he can express himself is through rage and anger. He is unable to rejoice in another man's victory, this fuels his anger and serves as a catalyst for further destruction. He is motivated by material things, and earthly pleasures. He does not know how to cultivate and appreciate balance. Nature does not speak to him because he is not at peace.

The sun blinds him instead of guiding him to the light, the truth, and toward right intentions. Every man makes his own choices, and these choices dictate who he becomes. Socrates once explained "that the vision of a clever, wicked man might be just as sharp as that of a philosopher. The problem lies in what he turns his sharp vision toward."

If he turns it toward the sun and the light he can find his own redemption, if he keeps turning to the shadows, he becomes a prisoner and will never be able to escape the dark cave.

Fortunate are those who are born in the light, free from the shackles of the cave. They are the bearers of bountiful gifts ready and open to share them with whoever is ready to receive them. They seek the truth, and it comes to them effortlessly.

*Those who are born in the light are never afraid of being who they **truly** are, with the rich man, the poor man, the sick man, the ignorant man, the intelligent man and especially the wicked man. The wicked man will go to great lengths and devise elaborate plans to cast shadows around the bearers of the light but will always fail because the light they carry can never be extinguished.*

Words Matter

I have done a lot of contemplation in my life. Having studied literature as an undergraduate student at McGill University in Montreal, I spent many days sitting at my favorite coffee shop reading novels, plays and poems while dreaming of becoming a writer. Eventually, I became a teacher and a creative writer. Writing has always been a huge part of who I am. I have been writing poems, stories, journals and documenting my life for as long as I can remember. Only recently have I truly understood the healing power this exercise has had on my life. Words have helped me heal. Somehow writing words down has allowed me the tremendous opportunity to transform my suffering and joys into art. The authenticity that comes from art, whatever form it takes, is truly transformative. It has the power to heal, inspire and provide a beautiful testimony of having lived a life. I am not a philosopher or a preacher, I am simply a lover of words and a passionate woman who is convinced that if you seek out your true potential and cultivate the unique gifts that only you can offer the world, you will have unlocked the most precious treasure of all: the incredible freedom that comes from self-expression and the peace that comes from reconciliation.

About the Author

Chiara Laricchiuta was born in Bathurst, New Brunswick and was raised by Italian immigrant parents in Montreal, Canada. She is a proud Canadian with very strong roots in her Italian culture. She is a college professor in Montreal, Canada. She has been teaching English for over 15 years. She has an undergraduate degree in English Literature from McGill University. She also has a graduate certificate in T.E.S.L from McGill University. In 2009, she obtained a Master's in Educational Studies from Concordia University. In addition to teaching, she has been writing creatively for over 20 years. Writing has always been her passion. In 2004, she completed a certificate in Journalism at Concordia University and began publishing her work in The Bridge Magazine, a magazine for new students at Concordia. Since then, some of her creative pieces and interviews have been published in magazines such as Accenti Magazine and Corriere Magazine, two cultural magazines highlighting the uniqueness of the Italian Canadian experience in Montreal.

When she isn't teaching or writing, Chiara loves to travel to Southern Italy and spends all her free time with her husband and young daughter.

www.ingramcontent.com/pod-product-compliance
Lightning Source LLC
Chambersburg PA
CBHW071217120626
46546CB00006B/2608